FEMINISTS ARE PASSING FROM OUR LIVES

Other books by Leslie McGrath:

Toward Anguish
Opulent Hunger, Opulent Rage
By the Windpipe
Out From the Pleiades

Feminists Are Passing

FROM OUR LIVES

POEMS

Leslie McGrath

THE WORD WORKS
WASHINGTON, D.C.

The Word Works
P.O. Box 42164
Washington, D.C. 20015
editor@wordworksbooks.org

Cover art: Tina Gibbard
Cover design: Susan Pearce Design
Author photograph: Andrea Stanton Photography

LCCN: 2018931396
ISBN: 978-1-944585-23-5

Acknowledgments

Grateful acknowledgment to the editors of the publications in which these poems, sometimes in earlier versions, first appeared:

Academy of American Poets (*poets.org*): "Ars Poetica"
Agni: "Mumblety Peg"
The Awl: "Bitterness in the Mouth" & "Rest in Warning"
Bennington Review: "Globalia"
Bridge Eight: "A Green So Green"
Cimarron Review: "Feminists Are Passing from Our Lives,"
        "Fearing the Mad," & "Paolo Has Left Me Three Apricots"
The Common: "Shook Music," "The Rhythm of Predation Is a
        Sine Wave," & "Encountering Franz Wright Along the Way"
Cutthroat: "Rage Bracelet," "The House Plant," & "Astonishment"
December Magazine: "Gift" & "Gifted"
Diaphanous Press: "Daydreaming in a Time of Panic" & "All the Goats"
Luxembourg Review: "Lines Scratched on a Bench"
Mead: "Daddy Longlegs"
Medical Journal of Australia: "An Insight"
Peacock Journal: "Baby Hippos, the Rain, and Other People's Pain,"
        "Billow," & "The Fleeting"
Poetry: "Nowhere Near Hudson's Bay"
Poetry Kanto (Japan): "Little Toy Horse" & "Liminalia"
The Punch: "Thirst" & "Agnostic"
Quaint: "After Hysterectomy"
Radius: "Two Poles and a Suicide"
Salon of the Refused: "Rejection Season"
Salamander: "A Music," "Litany," & "Brotherhood and the Strait Jacket"
Scythe: "Dr. Burckhardt Performs the First Lobotomy: Switzerland, 1886"
Slate: "The Mouth of the Mind"
Tilt-a-Whirl: "Madwoman's Ghazal" & "Her Dementia"
Truthdig.com: "Shock Wave"
Vox Populi: "An Anniversary," "Trump-wrung," & "A Winter Impulse"
Writers Resist: "Agnostic," "Just like Picking Flowers," & "Estrangement"
Yale Review: "Some Comfort in a Smaller Field of Vision"

"Surge / Wick / Raze" and "Luna Moth" appear in the anthology *Devouring the Green: Fear of a Human Planet,* Jaded Ibis Press, 2014.

"Stone Eclogue" appears in *Lay Bare the Canvas: New England Poets on Art,* 2014.

"View of a Neighbor's Bedroom in Winter" appears in the anthology *Still Life with Poem: Contemporary* Natures Mortes *in Verse* (ed. Jehanne Dubrow), Literary House Press, 2016.

A number of the poems in the collection were published as a chapbook entitled *By the Windpipe* by ELJ Press in 2014.

The first epigraph for this collection is from Betty Friedan's second generation feminist manifesto, *The Feminine Mystique.*

The second epigraph for this collection is from Elsa Svensson, also known as the daughter of necessity.

Sincere appreciation is given to the Beatrice Fox Auerbach Foundation (through the Greater Hartford Council for the Arts), the Vermont Studio Center, Hedgebrook, and the Rensing Center (Borseda, Italy). Their support was instrumental to the completion of this book.

My lasting gratitude to Sarah Gorham, Alfred Corn, Laura Orem, Kirby Gann, and the great Nancy White for their honest critiques and their friendship.

Contents

IV

The feminists had destroyed the old image of woman, but they could not erase the hostility, the prejudice, the discrimination that still remained.

—Betty Friedan, *The Feminine Mystique*

Dala horse, why do you speak through shadow?

—Elsa Svensson

For my daughters,
Carly & Elizabeth

Mumblety Peg

And when the truth about the emperor's clothes was revealed
the crowd convulsing with laughter at his flaccid gullibility
you noticed a young man easing the battered patty of a wallet
from a bald man's back pocket. Winking, the young man stuffed
the thing into the denim pouch strapped across his chest
then with two slim fingers tweezed a phone from the purse
gaping at a girl's shoulder. *What?* you sputtered, turning away
to look at something, anything, else.
You crouched to retrieve a pacifier from beneath
your toddler's stroller and found something else down there
like a pocket knife stuck in the dirt:
the word *accessory.* It pegged the pacifier; it pegged you.

Feminists Are Passing from Our Lives

It's wonderful how they jog
in two-toned gel-soled racing shoes
their yoga butts barely jiggling
in rosy spandex leggings.

I was there once. I felt
the brash *I've got it all*, I had
the uncomplicated beauty of the young
before the years peeled it from me

like flimsy wallpaper. In my memories
women's work was pin money
to pay for ballet lessons, summer camp;
suffering children, suffering filing jobs

suffering their husbands
who poured from the commuter train
gin-flushed and slurring. You who
I raised on *Our Bodies, Our Selves*

believe that feminism's as passé
as the sanitary napkin and the typewriter.
You roll your eyes and smirk
at my pleas not to become housewives.

I've seen that beast
hook its teeth on the cleverest PhD
and take her down for decades.
That won't happen to us

you say, *we've come too far.*
We're protected under the law
a majority, a force.
No. Not that big.

The Mouth of the Mind

In the garden this morning
I knelt to pinch the basil back
and found a baby rabbit
mild and untouchable as a baked potato.

He'll be my guest tonight
sitting at the table between you and me
wearing a double-breasted aluminum jacket.
In the salad bowl, an argument Bill and I had about money—
crisp Lincolns tossed in a lemon vinaigrette.
Frank's cancer's a Charlotte Russe
lying like a bullet casing on the counter.

All our daughters are grown, Sarah.
Why still cook when the chairs are empty?
The mind's eye's for imagining
but the mouth of the mind is a gullet

where our days empty out
—the everyday, the unbearable, the good—
and the night kitchen serves them up with iced mint tea
as fast as we can wash it all down.

Baby Hippos, the Rain, & Other People's Pain

There are worse ways to waste time
than watching YouTube videos of baby hippos

cavorting like fey gray beach balls
in huge water-filled tanks. Thanks to

recent improvements in underwater
photography we can see the hippo clearly above

and below the waterline. We see through rain
even though the brain knows each drop distorts

the light. It pieces the image together
into something close enough to real

that we recognize it. The pain of others
works this way too. It torques

beneath their skin, as near our own pain
as light is to a spark.

Ars Poetica

To have
even a
lotto chance

of getting
somewhere
within yourself

you don't quite know
but feel

To cling
to the periphery
through the constant

gyroscopic
re-drawing of its
provinces

To make
what Makers make

you must set aside
certainty

Leave it
a lumpy backpack
by the ticket window
at the station

Let the gentleman
in pleated khakis
pressed for time claim it

The certainty
not the poem.

You Times Two

The monitor thumps like a galloping horse
little boy heart little girl heart
as close as you'll ever be again
despite the shared day of your birth
you and you are due *now*
already working as a team
already linking the seven of us
out here in the waiting room our asses
killing us from the gritty plastic chairs
we've been sitting in all afternoon
a gray haired lady's knitting a striped
blanket for her great grandbaby
pink blue brown she's hedged gender
she's got it covered they're changing
shifts in maternity surgery your mother
ordered dinner hours ago your father
just sent a terse text: *it's time*
come already   unhinge   join us.

Gifted

She made not a sound

though they broke her clavicle
and folded her lengthwise to complete the birth.

After the doctor named her
syndrome, he asked her parents about their long-

range plans and passed her
to them as though she were already dead.

No, not dead:
instead, the third side of the family triangle.

Delicate and downyheaded
even when her breasts bloomed dutifully a handspan

above the diaper
that took two to change, she was a stranger to words

though her mouth
knew a smile as though she had invented it.

View of a Neighbor's Bedroom in Winter

Our neighbor's house is old and painted red
so long ago painted red that the clapboards peel
like sunburn though there's snow heaped on the roof.

Their bedside lamp is an old milk glass whimsy
the canvas shade cocked like a sailor's cap
as he squints at the dropping sun.

I settle my imagination
among the roses on the chenille bedspread
pulling from the stack on the illuminated table a book

I've already read, in which the heroine
lost her way by land, then made her way by water.

Laid her hard-won peace on a bed of fennel
on a fish-shaped platter
and when no one at the table touched her gift

she tipped it into the river.

Your home is home as long as you think it so
and no longer.

At the border of their yard and mine
under the icebound hedge
a rabbit hunkers like an anchor.

Gender Study

The house is dumb
with unreturned calls

Propped on the desk
my birthday card

their fading
signatures

I thumb
through a journal

& read another
poet's love letter
to his mother

Her sacrifices
& missteps
in every way like mine—

though forgiven.

Hell is furious daughters.

All the Goats

Sometime before midnight all the goats
sent away by those who wanted to distance themselves
from their sins and were lucky enough to have a goat
were roused from the rocky fields where they'd been sleeping
(in shame, thought the families, though they were wrong)
and were led back to town by a child that wore
a thin strip of cloth threaded through
the shank of a brass bell. The goats followed its song
through dark and stinking alleys back to the pens
and tired barns with roofs like saddles—
places where they'd known care. The child lay with them there
in one hay-padded place or another until daylight
then beckoned them back to the fields. Thus the families
continued to believe their distance from sin was intact
and that they were cleansed. And the goats said nothing.

Estrangement

Ripped
at the seams

the garment
laid out
for viewing

is a garment no longer

Child from mother
from sister from brother

Each an ostracism
ultimately
of the self

No punishment's
more intimate
than this

in which
she who suffers most
the absence, loses.

An Insight

Your heart's just fine

From an etherized twilight
I hear myself disagree: *I don't think so*

He snorts
Look at the screen to your left

and I'm face-to-heart
with my lifelong premonition
of an imminent end—

a cumulonimbus locomotive barrels silently
in place
as my dye-darkened arteries hang on for dear life

Matias Järvinen Is Out on the Ice

on a northern lake
in February
his canvas day pack
held fast by an ice
pick, a folding bench
and a dry suit scant
insulation from
six centimeters
of dim translucence
through which he's augered
a hole a giant
sommelier might bore.
Into this gelid
distance he has slipped
a lone filament
a line of prayer
for perch, arctic char
for a mind as clear
as the clear sublime.

Agnostic

She with
her sac
of eggs
strung between
curved wall
& clapper
doesn't know
her world's
a bell.

Encountering Franz Wright Along the Way

I had been dawdling I don't know how long
In the placid dark after the rash of day had receded.
I found an anvil-shaped stone in a field overlooking the road
And thinking I was alone, made audible the speech
I knew not to share with any person for fear of frightening them.
I lay back on that stone, turning away from the trees, away
From their ceaseless industry, toward the everything I could not see
But pretended to. He appeared on the smooth cheek of the sky
The raw edge of a raw edge, alarming the stars into stillness.
"Don't be so much at the mercy of things," he boomed
But as I began to utter a polite *fuck off*, the sky behind him
The night sky, flashed emerald. This, his lucid recognition
Of the unabating shame made flesh in me. If he said more
Before he meteored away, I don't recall. All I heard was mercy.

II

Liminalia

Begin as November
begins: vague chill
and the sense
that what came before
returns listless
as though tired
of its own bordering
nature. Neither one
nor the other
neither bridge nor river.

Thirst

Up from our slack river fox tracks a path
past an apple slick parched bees now occupy.

Drought has poached the tomato plants
strangled the new-planted dogwood
brought low the foragers. Poor foragers.

August, you have done your job
of exhausting us

all but the fox
who hurries to her fate.
Her fine red mettle level as water.

Daydreaming in a Time of Panic

So you have found me heartsick, curled under
the throw someone's grandmother crocheted
and that I bought at Goodwill because I'm mindful and adjunct.

I'm not doing nothing here. I'm calculating the angle
of light that casts a long and chilling shadow
onto the largest screen on earth: millions of turned backs

of tweeters, texters, and trolls hell-bent
over devices designed to connect but which only sift
self from self and will continue to do so until

someone with a working moral compass, someone
who senses the hypnotic sleep of history coming round
and round again writes ALARM! ALARM!

gigantic and trance-piercing on the wind no blanket
will protect me from. These hands are busy
with my rosary of hurts, but oh if they weren't!

What would I become? Bell that warns the world.
What have I become? Talking mynah bird.

Luna Moth

I last saw one decades ago.
There were nine or ten that July night
moon-green and big as dinner plates
some affixed to the doorscreen, others hovering
like slow applause at the edge of the sphere of light
cast by the hall lamp. Both drawn and threatened
by what we've made to illumine our human way
they were gone by daybreak.

Yesterday morning we found one poised on the lantern.
A tragicomic beauty: his tiny Nosferatu head ironically
without a mouth
the false eyes on his wings meant to scare predators away
could've been cigarette burns.

As a child I might've said he was the son of a barn swallow
and a cabbage leaf, of a fairy queen and a kite.
Ten years ago, the son of a coat hanger and a theater curtain
a golf umbrella and pinking shears
or a jet and a twenty dollar bill.

How long before we liken every natural thing
to its technologic spawn? No singleton, no swarm
just a pixelated image
I once saw of a moth—mild, defiant, and doomed.

Stone Eclogue

We've walked all the way to Christmas
the dog and I, between stone walls
and up to the old well, turning home
at the badge of blue lichen
on a stone at the driveway's end.

It was fifty years in the stitching
but nothing can wait like stone.

These walls mark the old roads
families would travel on Sundays to church
or to sell the wool sheared from the sheep
herded into the stone corral behind the barn.

Such stones, natural-squared and bricklike
were so plentiful, the men
who cleared these hills for farming
stacked them higher than their horses' heads.

Heaped in a stoneyard's lowest corner
lies the unusable, the too-small, the oval
good for neither chimney nor wall, tossed
over the shoulder as refuse.
Stone potatoes
were a cruel joke in the years
when famine threatened even the steadiest.

There were no crops but stone.

On a hillside there's another yard of stone
hidden in a stand of slender beeches—

Aaron and Elihu Bennett, twins dead in their teens
eleven Bennett infants, most gone before their naming
Abagail Bennett, who lived to eighty-nine

in a house built two dozen years
before Revolutionary winds blew
through the frame and lath.

Cold spirits swirling around the granite spine of the house
a fire ever-lit in its three hearths
for cooking, washing, warmth. Hearthstones hewn
from a massive gray tablet
by a stonemason whose name has faded
from the household ledger.

He split stone with a star-tipped iron rod
long as his forearm
and a heavy mallet, playing a xylophone
of feathers and wedges until the stone gave up its singing
and fell open like a family bible.

What the mason left lives in the stone he worked
as the women of the house, tenders of the kettle
and the spit, live in the chimney flue's thick creosote
as the builders of walls
live in the miles of stacked stones
shouldering the roads, making peace
through boundary, running unseen
through the winter woods, dissolving by weather
by lichens, by degrees
as all things do.

Surge / Wick / Raze

1. Surge

Under the strobes mounted on their camo'd Jeeps
National Guardsmen seem to wobble as they check
my ID before waving me into the dark.
This is not my neighborhood. I live further inland
and have returned to watch my mother's house
after the water moved where it never had before.
Where we never thought it would. The lamp
in her front hall the still point of illumination
as the tide backlaps through dark yards, dark houses
back over the berms the town built years ago
back into the Sound's shallow basin.
An isosceles of yellow police tape flutters from an oak
to the minivan it crushed, as though what happened here
was just a Mischief Night toiletpapering. This is not
my neighborhood. Tomorrow we'll find starfish
in the climbing hydrangea trained along the fence.
The stench of something between death and heating oil
will assert itself with the sun. Now the urge to ebb
to recoil in apology for the avoidable
for the unfixable, for the spitting wires dangling from trees
for the ruined photographs that would have given
our lives a chance of being remembered
by those who follow, for the poisoned
backyard gardens and the last puckered tomatoes
on blackened vines in this neighborhood not mine.

2. Wick

After water
rushes
horizontal
the wicking
begins. Think
of a flooded
house as
thirsty drinker
sipping
through
millions of stiff
straws
up beam and
plasterboard
up curtain and
wallpaper.
Like a candle's
capillary action
channeling fuel
to flame
wicked water
erupts into
mold black mold.

3. Raze

The scales are tipping. Let them tip.
Resist the urge
to right the ship, let the sea
have its due and the earth have its due.

History may appear asleep
but it is awake, and moving.

Let the hands of consequence set to work
on the unbuilding of beam, board, pane
of stainless and automatic.

Let it topple, flatten, rot.
Let the movement be horizonward.

Time is coming, has come.

Let the harrier nest in these reeds again
intent, listening for scurriers.

Let this be salt marsh, hunting plain, birthplace and grave
not a neighborhood.

Rest in Warning

In the dark before morning lay the living in their beds
and lay we the dead in ours. Each earth-lidded terminus
not a chamber of rest, but a listening ear to the past.

The dead are with you, difficult as this is to believe.
We know how quickly you turn from mourning
back to the distractions you stretch from hour to hour.

You buy green mangoes from the street vendor
and pink tulips from the corner bodega. Finally alone
in your apartment, the bolt slid against strangers,

you collapse in exhaustion. No news, you vow,
no devices all the long weekend. The cat nuzzles
your tulips and pushes the vase off the kitchen table.

You can't get her off the furniture. Here in the yard
at the edge of the Old Town, there's no keeping
the living out. You are our news, constant and uninvited,

opening the iron gate to stroll among our rows.
You place pebbles atop granite markers, whisper our names
as though we can no longer speak. We speak

in the dark before morning when the vandals come
tagging hate and toppling headstones. They give us voice.
Each thud's a certain warning that the past is never gone.

As long as the beaver slaps her tail on the pond's surface,
as long as the rabbit stomps his hind leg, listen.
This sound is the only sound we make.

Stone Wall

: stone was once loose matter : litter : stone as hazard : error :

stone as nuisance : a farmer's vexation : stones in a field

thrown aside in field-clearing : stone piled into cairns : stone

on stone : stone called feldspar : called basalt : called granite :

stones the little ice age heaved up like crops : flat stones

& square : cobblestones & capstones : stack : stack : stack

stones scuttled against the fenceline : stone as fenceline :

as corral : stone as foundation : habitat stone : stone

as canvas : stone as yardstick : as chimney & hearth :

stone as judge : stone the weft of history, human & stone:

At a Roadside Stand in Salem, CT

I bought a half-peck
of Macouns
and a pumpkin
whoopie pie
big as a pumpkin

I'd pulled in
for a closer look
at the crowd
in the parking lot—

horses frozen
in mid-buck
black gryphons squatting
in a sparrow line

and backed against
the chain link
the Virgin Mary
leaning hard
on the Statue of Liberty.

An Anniversary

(Newtown, CT, December 14, 2012)

Cue the half-mast flags sagging
eleven listless days before Christmas
and the entreaties to return to our senses.

It takes nearly a month, an advent calendar
of griefs, to pay homage to each of our twenty-six.

And in other towns, other states, other guns,
other massacres...

The age of murder is upon us.
What is there to do but straighten our shoulders
and dip our heads for this moment of silence
efficiently, indifferently, like a cat
washing blood from her face?

Shock Wave

(Boston Marathon, April 2013)

Blow black powder and shrapnel blow
    a deathwind

then follows another kind of detonation—
    this one inward.

In the brain's chapel
one pearled sulcus is aroused by sudden fear
while others snap into lockdown.

There are moments when survival depends on suspicion
and the mind's ear turns vigilante

gum heard as gun
coffee heard as coffin
dread as dead

There are moments that become eras
Like this one   like this.

Globalia

Global Wealth Inequality: an irony

The mirror shatters. The window it had covered shows every person inside what is outside—

Worms wriggle in a rain puddle. Smoke rises from the baker's oven.

And every person outside what is inside—

Billionaires, cheeks pressed against the walls, with only enough space to jingle the change in their deep pockets.

*

Global Warming: a prediction

No worms because no rain puddle because no rain
No smoke because no fuel because no trees because no rain

*

Global Politics: a warning

Threat threat   threat threat
boom.

*

Global Uncertainty: an answer

I am sure
of very
little. Is
this not
wisdom?

III

Nowhere Near Hudson's Bay

Toggle me up
on one last vanity flight
half drunk on a screw-top *frizzante*.
It takes a hell of a lot more to get me here
than it did when I had beauty, boys
when bedding me was the easy way to know me.

Don't tuck me in
so tight. I'm not your grandma.
This rough blanket
its green red yellow indigo stripes
I traded for a perfectly warm beaver pelt.

Fly me once more
over my disloyal youth
and its hangdog slavering over men
whom age has de-sexed right along with me.
They broadcast impotent outrage
from aluminum tablets.
I collect speculums with Bakelite handles
arranging them by size
though it no longer matters.

Plunder, Plunder

When I was young I'd go where urges led me
then trail contrition all the way home

I wanted to fuck the world
and I tried

picked every lock licked every prick

plunder plunder
was my song

I never got tired of privateering
but the cleanup was a bitch

dozens of sticky beer bottles
rolling around in the bed
of my pickup truck
a Ford STD

Are you a good feminist? you ask

That'll take a lifetime to answer
because feminism is exorcism
of the old ways, of the old things

and every possession seems demonic
when you're demonized

for treasuring the red ahoy
pulsing deep within your pirate gut.

After Hysterectomy

In heaven's infinite space for souls, deep in its overgrown back acres there must be stockpiled all that was shed in childhood (milk teeth, tonsils, appendixes) until the spirits housed in them are ready to let go the rest of the body. A platform, a reunion place. And nearby, a medical midden, because even the disposed-of is returned to mama or papa. There awaits the prodigal tissue from nose jobs and knee replacements, kidney, lung and liver transplants. Tons of cartilage and gelid bellyfat iglooed in the gloom. Dozens of pallets of foreskins piled like neatly-folded opera gloves gives the place an electricity of recent applause. But only for the wombs dangling like earrings from the castaway ribs of the waist-obsessed. Only for the wombs—because no matter her race or religion, no matter her intelligence or age, a woman surrenders what she's told she must surrender.

Rage Bracelet

Women create the beast to know
the depth of their desire

>*every prison wants a warden*
>*every tablecloth a stain*

A matched set of bruises
at the collarbone   round the wrist

>*every guru wants a devotee*
>*every amulet a chain*

Women forgive the beast and learn
the depth of their despair

>*every landscape wants a shadow*
>*every abattoir a drain*

Feminist Question

(an erasure of Gloria Steinem's *New York Times*
editorial in support of Bill Clinton, 1998)

All the swirling around the White House,
President Clinton. Another double standard.

The President behaved with insensitivity.
Expected? I don't think so.

Journalist: Suggest he resign.
Forget it.

Accusations against Clinton,
against Bob Packwood, Clarence Thomas.

The President's favorable ratings among women.
Sexual behavior 30 years ago: no means yes.

Sexual harassment: when someone's will
has been violated. "No" as an answer.

Look at the most damaging allegations,
old enough to be Monica Lewinsky's mother.
A family tragedy.

You might be skeptical
but you think, "I believe the women."

At least until we know more. More.

If the allegations are true
the President is guilty of sexual harassment,
gross and reckless.

Never again. In other words, no.

Paula Jones refused,
suffered psychological damage.
Allegations, accusations.

Accept rejection. It occurred
in the regular workplace,
where it could not be avoided.

The women had to go to work every day
knowing sexual humiliation would await, reduce.

Monica Lewinsky's case: Yes means yes?
The power imbalance is relevant to sexual harassment.

President Clinton lied under oath.

We have a responsibility to tell the truth,
as we are doing now.

Some Comfort in a Smaller Field of Vision

Happy not-seeing
The long sweep to the river
White lilac has bloomed
It catches my thoughts of you
Before they float east, griefward

Her Dementia

I walk the earth I have forgotten
I speak a language lost to me.
This wind is *cello*, this woman *cotton*.
I walk the earth and have forgotten

which memory's mine and which is not
and who was she I used to be.
I walk the earth. I have forgotten.
I speak a language. I'm lost to me.

Gift

If he could speak and hadn't lost the strength
to raise his hand above his heart
or turn to greet her as she rushed in,
tossing her red scarf over the chair,
he'd thank her for providing him what he most missed:
her commonplace art—
the arcs her fingers traced as she held his head and washed his hair.

Astonishment

Here you are in Italy, leaning on a gate
a poetry tote looped over an arm.

You wear blue: blue coat, blue scarf
draped in the way of a European woman
your long hair untamed in the way of a northern Californian.

I call you friend, beloved friend
though you wouldn't recognize me
in the grocery store if I turned to ask you
how to choose a sweet melon.

We met on the coldest day Vermont had seen in ages
as you stamped snow
on the braided rug with what I've learned to think of
as your everyday astonishment
at the shattering cold and its glassy scent,
mittens hissing on the radiator, all of it.

That was years ago
when our letters were delivered by hand
when there was time before we'd grow old

me grading essays on my porch
you in constant orbit, audience to audience—

London and Umbria, Krakow and Seoul.

I'd know you, Dear One
even if I never saw you again.

I'd know you the way a bluebird
not having seen her kin since learning flight
knows her song.

A Winter Impulse

Two waxwings at the suet cake.
One pecks, the other picks what falls. It takes
a winter impulse: work together to get through.
What if it had been that way with you?

The House Plant

Long ago, soon after you lost your first tooth,
we watched your father re-pot his spider plant
in the garden shed. Propping the door open

with a sack of potting mix, he bent down
and gathered the leaves in a kind of loose ponytail,
shaking until the pot let go the tangled roots.

With one hand I've held your hair like this
and cupped your clammy forehead with the other
to comfort you a little as you vomited.

He must have done these things too, through
stomach bugs and flu, experiments with booze
(and more I won't go into) in your furious adolescence.

He sliced open the bag of soil, half-filling
two terra cotta pots, then eased the roots apart
as I would a knot caught in your My Little Pony comb,

dunked them in a bucket of fertilized water
(he always had a gift for strong beginnings)
then tucked the soil around them like goodnight.

All the incantations at the altar come down to this:
Do for each other. And I suppose we did, through you.
Can a child feel wholly cherished by one parent at a time?

The clump I took in the divorce now crowds a window,
its pot white-furred with lime and cracks resembling hieroglyphs
in a language none of us can remember.

One bump with the vacuum, one infelicitous turn
toward the winter sun and the pot would fall to pieces.
This the last shared thing—aside from you, our daughter.

Lines Scratched on a Bench

Along the northernmost tip of the Blue Ridge we edged ledges
narrow as hem binding on the mountain's granite skirt.

Shaky-legged after an hour of up/over/through
a rock scramble remaindered by the Ice Age

I found a bench, a hand-hewn cedar whimsy,
with these words carved into its soft gray seat—

I do not think you will take care of me when I am old.
You have me afraid to age.

The hours it must have taken with his pocketknife
to leave those doubts as far as they could be left.

The hours it must have taken in tremorous descent—
summoning the resolve to stay

or accepting the letting-go.

Paolo Has Left Me Three Apricots

On the sill of the first floor window he's left them
on a cool shelf of shade
at the yellow stone house I've rented for July.

Were it not for Paolo and a few others
building up their winter woodpiles
and hanging laundry on Saturdays
I'd think this village was abandoned

though a few times a week it's visited by men
who sell milk and fish and other necessaries
out of their cars. Loyal as old lovers
they toot their horns to announce their arrival
at every plaster jumble barnacled here
in the mountains of Lunigiana
the chalice-shaped place between grand Tuscany
and the vineyard steppes of Liguria.

Unreplenished by children, these villages
have grown frail. I watch modest women
in modest dresses and serious shoes
zigzag stiffly from the piazza
up the laddered stone steps to the church
as the beginnings of the Sunday meal—
the pot of sauce, the pasta drying on wooden racks
the tender zucchini blossoms
wait in the dark kitchens of their empty houses.

This is a vertical life
not only in its perpendicular geography
but in its economy.
What is owned is used, saved, bartered, lent
in the old way, when there was little difference
between neighbor and family.

The local currency? What is made here
grown here or hauled up the mountain.
Three apricots equals an afternoon's happiness.

Rejection Season

In January the winter river grinds itself down
like a Ticonderoga pencil in a desk-mounted
sharpener, ice heaving down and down and downstream
a logjam of the sloughed, the shell casings of
a Hellful of editors who use this margin of the year
to send volleys of stiffly written rejections
thank you for letting us have a look to email addresses
like poetjanedoe@hotmail and johndoenovelist@yahoo
and my own awkward lastname.firstname@gmail
thereby crushing yet another year's accretion
of wobbily built-up confidence that I've written
the unrejectable, the great leap forward, the poem
that will pry open the clamped hearts of the citizenry
to the foul suffering and injustice we paddle in
all the while thinking *I could swim out of this
if I wanted to* because I've read that to not be taken
by a rip current you must swim parallel to shore
and then I remember there are no rip currents
in rivers, just layers of currents and the forgotten
submerged, the water's own unconscious
you could call it: each squashed soda can
skipped rock, stolen bike and every sodden
paper boat folded, named, launched, and sunk
after we've had a look, after we've all had a look.

IV

To Madness

If you had come majestic, sweeping in
like wind-driven rain and allowed me
to slip the pink slicker from its hook in the back hall
to cover myself

if you had been candid about your cruelty
and the casual way you'd pin me by the windpipe
replacing my words for yours

if you had been a reliable adversary
and abided rules, a schedule
that followed any regional logic

but you came vague, a nakedness
and you stayed for years, a stain.

Litany

Each day's a train bound for Calgary, St. Paul, Santa Fe,
its flickering windows a foreign film.

The doors will never open. But the tracks will beckon.
You'll lay your body across them, feeling for the hum,

the electric indelible, that connects all beings,
you've heard. No train will come, so you'll let it go.

You'll get chilly, get up, drive home and call a friend.
She'll take you to the hospital. In you'll go

through doors that lock audibly at your back.
They'll want your sharps (nail file, shoelaces). You'll let them go.

They'll give you a diagnosis. Another. Another.
They'll prescribe Prozac, which will work, then stop.

You'll go through four more medications to find a transitory peace.

Another patient, your confidant, will turn quiet.
You'll find her hanging from the shower bar. You'll watch her go

out on a gurney, the same way she arrived, in a bag this time.
You'll get with the program: music therapy, art therapy, family therapy.

You'll gain weight, insight. You'll get a discharge date
then begin to wonder what you've missed—the new television season,

elections, fall fashions, the body count. They've let you go
from your job. They've filled your spot in the choir.

Most of your friends, too, will be gone
but this will be done in a way you discover incrementally

through a series of unmet glances,
unreturned calls and other small dishonors.

Your husband will remove his ring. *I didn't sign up for this.*

You'll hire an attorney. He'll hire an attorney.
You'll lose custody of your children

and God help you, you'll let them go
to the fitter parent, the more competent one,

the parent who did not go through this.

You'll make a fresh start, buy a house
in another town and you'll drink your evening wine

but you'll let that lonely pleasure go too far.
This too, you will let go.

You'll find a lover. He'll bring his hammer and his temper.
After you argue he'll make a bonfire of your furniture.

Standing barefoot at your own door
you'll watch it all go—spark to ash.

You'll go back to bed for a day, a week
then a cold season of days will flicker past the panes,

past you, alone on that familiar platform
now overgrown with vines. You will take hold

of one and pull it up. You'll pull another, another.
Soon you'll stand between the mass of weeds

and a cleared place. This is where you'll plant
mint and nasturtium and watch them grow

thickly fragrant over the borders. You'll make
a friend, paint your bedroom, go to church.

Late one afternoon on the porch
you'll feel an easing of resentments

toward those who have not suffered,
toward those to whom suffering is invisible

as you let go and let go and let go.

Shook Music

Follow me, Imagineers! We'll make noise
from these dread instruments, shook music
loud as the hell we've climbed from, visible
only to the *i* in piano, the eye in the oboe.

We'll hoist a cheesecake by an iron hook
and swing blindly at it with our puny claws.
We'll howl under its influences, meet cute
fuck, and forget before the trembling's done.

Once finished, we'll flame out, God or no.
Still, we'll take our dead with us, our legions
with us, and because there's always
room for piety, our greatness with us.

Little Toy Horse

a standing
lesson
in the art
of tension

wooden bead head   wooden
bead body   wooden bead
legs   vascular elastic

but press a thumb
against the bottom panel—

all fall down.

Daddy Longlegs

He's a thimble of pins
a skeletal bumbershoot
lounging like a pasha
in loose hammocked silks
still. still.   until
some unwitting winged
thing, enrapt
        missteps
trap   wrap
a neat fatal bite.
       Presto!
Daddy's got a mummy.

Two Poles and a Suicide

Look how her dark eyes smile
black as her last night.
Her photo's curled, yellow.
A chip. A chip to shoulder.

She was sorceress, sorely loved,
linger of mint, a plea left
on too many answering machines
when there were answering machines.
Everything is smaller now.

She was, she said, slave
to a slave to fame, a lover
of white elephants, black
pearls. Nomad in a fatherless
land, she traveled from
pole to pole until
left at the altar of exhaustion,
a dendritic tripwire
strung from attic to basement,
she died in the dining room
and she had company.

A tour guide, she was,
not to the hell of her own
despair, blithe and capricious,
but to the imagined hell
even mention of her name
now takes us to. We are not
to be blamed for going there.
We are not to be blamed
for going there.

Billow

Late May and the scent of beach primrose overwhelms the sea's brine. We've walked single file through morning fog onto a little beach hoping to not be seen doing a thing that comforts us, a thing we think may be illegal. We're seven poets. Eight if you count the plastic bag of ashes her estranged husband holds far enough away so that it doesn't bump against his hip at every step. She was a poet, a fine one; now four pounds of ashes. He rolls up his pants to the knee, wades in, then leans toward the deeper water and pours some of her out. He offers her to us and I'm aware of holding my breath as I plunge my fingers into her ash and bone. Her goneness. I tip a handful of her into the water, the element she wrote about with the kind of obsessiveness poets tend to be proud of. Cloudiness expands there. No dissipation, just a flourishing opacity. A few of us use our hands as paddles, helping stir her in like vodka into juice. Slowly she disperses, the billow of shifting excuses, unanswered calls, and last-minute cancellations she'd thrown around herself over the last five years. She drank. She drank passionately. Exclusively. Dangerously. She drank too much. She drank herself away from our concern, our offers of help, and finally, away from our repulsion. Under the ripples she drifts finely away.

The Fleeting

It falls   as light
from a banished thought
will sometimes
settle   redworn & carefingered
close by the newly dead
who   not quite still with us
      & not quite gone
could judge   knowing the edges
of our crucial illusories
                        but don't.

Fearing the Mad

This one shrieked when the crazyman approached.
This one turned her back.
This one shook her head *No* when the crazyman asked
for some spare change.
And this one said *They should lock that man up*
for the rest of his days.

This one called the cops when the crazylady upstairs
walked out the door in her slip.
This one called the cops when she entered his store.
He checked the shelves when she left.
And this one said *They should lock that lady up*
for the rest of her days.

This one said her kids couldn't play with the boy
who talked of his invisible friend.
This one said the girl who banged her head against the wall
shouldn't be in school.
And this one said *Lock them up for their safety*
for the rest of their days.

This one drinks a fifth of gin each night.
This one ties her mother to a chair
when she goes to work.
This one watches nothing but violent porn.
And these ones say *Stay out of our private lives*
for the rest of our days.

Dr. Burckhardt Performs the First Lobotomy, Switzerland, 1886

Enter the patient.
Enter his babbling   his threatening gestures.

See his mother kiss him on the cheek as she releases his arm.

See the assistant ask him to sit on the sturdy table
      —he pours clear liquid into a cloth
      —he holds it to the patient's face
        while cupping the back of his head.

See the patient flail, then slump sideways.
    He is now asleep, says the assistant, *and feels no pain.*

See the assistant tie the patient's arms and legs tightly
      wrists to table   ankles to table.

Enter Dr. Gottlieb Burckhardt,
    famous for his theory that a disordered mind
        equals a disordered brain.

    He has stated   *It is better to do something than nothing.*

        Today he makes good on that claim
          by surgically removing madness.

See the tools laid out on a small table
      side by side by gleaming side
and the piles of folded white cloth.

Here is an awl   here three saws of varying sizes
      there, near the basin, a long-handled scoop
        like that for ice cream or other confections.

Let the instruments be sharp   let them be free of rust   let them be clean.

Over the patient's soft snoring, Dr. Burckhardt speaks to an
audience of surgeons:

> *Gentlemen, today I shall give great relief to this poor fellow,*
> *who has since the age of twenty suffered increasingly*
> *from agitation, disturbances of vision and smell, and the*
> *erroneous belief that he is the son of Czar Alexander II. I shall*
> *create a ditch in the temporal lobe, removing from his brain that*
> *which causes his mind such suffering, leaving him mentally free.*

While the doctor is speaking, the assistant shaves
                          with avidity and a straight razor
                                    the patient's head.

The careful Dr. Burckhardt washes his hands in a basin of cool water.
          (He has read a recent monograph by a Dr. Lister in which
          invisible factors called "germs" may be responsible for
          disease.)
          He measures 6.5 centimeters over the ear.
          He nods to his assistant   who holds the head   still.

Without hesitation he applies the awl.

He is in.

Let Dr. Burckhardt's hands be steady
let his assurance be constant as the hum of bees
                          in the field outside the open window
let his luck exceed his confidence.

See him pick up the saw with the shortest blade
          —he inserts its tip into the hole in the skull
          —he draws the saw back   but it catches.
                    The blade's too fine.

See him remove the blade   slowly   out   it   comes
                          and with it   a trickle of pink.

79

—he grasps the handle of a more substantial saw
—he inserts the blade two centimeters deep into the patient's head
—he yanks the blade back.

With this motion   a sound
                between an animal's wail
                and the *whuff!* of a steam engine.

                        A meek wisp of something   (is it smoke?)
                                rises from the skull
                                        like a wish.

There is an hour of loud sawing.   Dr. Burckhardt's shoulders
                                are stiff from his exertions
                and his hands shake as he picks up the scoop
                        to dislodge the ragged circle of bone
                                the circumference of a candle.

The assistant finds a few clean cloths   checks the patient's breathing
                        and steadies the head

as Dr. Burckhardt scoops the matter gingerly
                from the bowl of the skull.   It is the light gray
                                of a field mouse
                                        yet has the consistency
                        of one of Mrs. Burckhardt's fruit puddings.
                        It is weighed at just over 2.6 grams.

Dr. Burckhardt is pleased—   surely he has excised enough
                to render an improvement in the patient's symptoms
                                        if the patient lives.

                More quickly now   on the left side of the skull:
                        awl   saw   scoop   staunch   snore

The audience has enough time for tea   through much of the third hour
        as the wound is packed   and the patient rises groggily
            into consciousness.

In the coming months, all will know

that this procedure   Burckhardt's second   was a success
                                    as psychiatric successes go:

        despite some loss of fluency in his speech
        and the need for a daily nap
        the patient will grow roses   and grow old
                    living quietly with his mother.

Brotherhood and the Strait Jacket

In Mr. Rodriguez's high school World History class, a lecture about the crushing stress on ordinary citizens— through poor harvests, through taxes on the very salt and wheat needed for bread, through limiting their right to work a trade—takes his students to the hungry city of Paris and its muddy neighboring villages, where the middle class rises up, crying *Liberté, égalité, fraternité!* Mid-morning, Rodriguez splits his class into two groups: serfs and nobility. A single saltless lunch after serving the nobles their burgers and cupcakes was all the serfs needed to get behind a concept like brotherhood. *That* idea came late to the French Revolution. Maybe it came in 1790 from an upholsterer named Guilleret after visiting Bicêtre Hospital, where the elderly and insane, the sick and the outlaw were housed together outside Paris. A shrieking heap of human refuse which attendants did their best to feed and clean, to protect from the predators among them. This was done, yes, with chains. Irons and chains. Who was Guilleret visiting? Was it the clang of chains throughout the ward that sparked his idea? Their constricting length? The putrid sores on wrists and ankles? Brotherhood. These were not animals. Swaddling calms a squalling infant, why not a shrieking adult? Rodriguez learned in his first year how soothing was the balm of his hand on a student's shoulder. Guilleret sewed from canvas a shirt, a *camisole de force*, whose sleeves wrapped round the waist and were tied behind the back in a dignified self embrace, as if to say *I am here. See me: your brother.*

The Rhythm of Predation Is a Sine Wave

Between predator and prey it winds

like a whip-crack in slow motion.
The time has come to praise the prey

who fill the guts of the never-satisfied
for whom winning is all, and nothing.

Praise the squeak and the telling tremble.
Praise their begging and their shame.

Praise their jugular fullness, the sweet red pulse
the ever-open spigot of their submission.

Let go the lamentations. Let go the pity.

All hail the awkward and the addlebrained
the boneheaded, the broken-down, the bonkers.

All hail the cracked and the cuckoo
the lame, the lunatic, and the losers.

Here's to the nutjobs, the outcasts
the peculiar and the unhinged.

For them, the wedgie and the booby prize
the tar, the feathers and the narrow rail.

History is written on the vellum of their bellies.

Just like Picking Flowers

The almond wears a thin corduroy vest
that cannot protect the nut. The skin

of a ripe peach peels like a second
degree burn. The oyster

clenches even as
we break its nacreous wings
at the hinge to get at the meat.

When the mushroom man appeared with baskets
braceleted up to his elbow
that shudder morning

he said the girls knew what to do (the best
mushrooms grew on the north sides of trees)

It was just like picking flowers, he said
and girls were good at that. But the boys

he'd have to show.

He led the boys away

    (on his knees he showed them)
    (with their pants down he showed them)

and we girls filled our baskets   we knew what to do
though we did not know   we did not know.

This was how he separated us.

Bitterness in the Mouth

When did the word
for *stranger* and
bitterness in the mouth
come to mean
a kind of audacity?
I've seen in some
men a distinctly
American gall—
they glide over
the rest of us
in their socks like
we're one long hallway
and they're late
for a banquet in
their honor. Shameless
they tell us they've done us
a favor. We needed
polishing. They needed
traction. Frotteurs
work like this—
we come away wondering
if we've been
screwed, gorge rising
as a hard little stranger
gets off.

A Green So Green

At the beginning of the end of depression
color returned like a promise

made by someone who loved you
while you were a torn casing rattling soundlessly,
the nymph snatched up by a bird long flown.

You'd felt the kidnap, quick surgery
and though you never saw the bird
you knew the rough curve of its wing
was red.

You knew the emptiness
it flew into and into was mild sky blue

and the fast-retreating landscape
you couldn't remember caring about
a green so green you called it ransom.

Resound

The flower of a weed is a flower
An arm in a cast, an arm
A person in prison, a person
Harm done unawares is still harm.

Some things we hear once and remember
Only some things forgotten are gone
A refrain is music worth repeating
The echo of song is song.

A Music

When at last I knew my illness had no lasting shadow
only the rising of light under lintel
you could have spun me silver
tricked thin as fish pins
and wedged me tight within that windpipe
some call God.

I'd've become harmonica. Still could.

Notes

"Surge / Wick / Raze" is for the environmentalist Joy Shaw.

"The Fleeting" and "Billow" are in memory of Wendy Battin.

"Two Poles and a Suicide" is in memory of Reetika Vazirani.

"Shook Music" is built around a phrase from Norman Rush's *Subtle Bodies*: "you can't lift a cheesecake with an iron hook."

"Feminists Are Passing from Our Lives" borrows from Phil Levine's poem "Animals Are Passing from Our Lives."

In "Rage Bracelet" the line "they create the beast to know the depth of their desire" is from Deborah Digges's poem "Anna Akhmatova."

"Her Dementia" is based on Milosz's line "I walk the earth I am forgetting" from his poem, "Forget."

"Fearing the Mad" is inspired by Donald Justice's poem "Counting the Mad."

"Resound" is inspired by Jane Hirshfield's poem "Sheep."

About the Author

Leslie McGrath is the author of two full-length poetry collections, *Opulent Hunger, Opulent Rage* (Main St Rag, 2009) and *Out From the Pleiades* (Jaded Ibis Press, 2014), and two chapbooks, *Toward Anguish* (Providence Athenaeum, 2007) and *By the Windpipe* (ELJ Press, 2014).

Winner of the Pablo Neruda Prize for Poetry and the Gretchen Warren Prize from the New England Poetry Club, she has been awarded residencies at Hedgebrook and the Vermont Studio Center, as well as funding from the Connecticut Commission on the Arts and the Beatrice Fox Auerbach Foundation. She has served on the board of the James Merrill House and the poetry advisory committee at the Hill-Stead Museum in Farmington, CT.

McGrath's poems and interviews have been published widely, including in *Agni, Poetry, The Academy of American Poets, The Writer's Chronicle,* and *The Yale Review*. She teaches creative writing at Central Connecticut State University and founded The Tenth Gate Prize to recognize the work of mid-career poets. Currently she also serves as judge for the Yeats Poetry Prize.

She lives in Essex, CT, with her husband Bill Taylor, a shipwright.

About the Artist

Tina Gibbard is an oil painter whose work explores psychological situations and connections. She lives and works in London.

About The Word Works

Since its founding in 1974, The Word Works has steadily published volumes of contemporary poetry and presented public programs. Its imprints include The Washington Prize, The Tenth Gate Prize, The Hilary Tham Capital Collection, and International Editions.

Monthly, The Word Works offers free literary programs in the Chevy Chase, MD, Café Muse series, and each summer it holds free poetry programs in Washington, D.C.'s Rock Creek Park. Word Works programs have included "In the Shadow of the Capitol," a symposium and archival project on the African American intellectual community in segregated Washington, D.C.; the Gunston Arts Center Poetry Series; the Poet Editor panel discussions at The Writer's Center; and Master Class workshops, and a writing retreat in Tuscany, Italy.

As a 501(c)3 organization, The Word Works has received awards from the National Endowment for the Arts, the National Endowment for the Humanities, the D.C. Commission on the Arts & Humanities, the Witter Bynner Foundation, Poets & Writers, The Writer's Center, Bell Atlantic, the David G. Taft Foundation, and others, including many generous private patrons.

An archive of artistic and administrative materials is kept in the Washington Writing Archive housed in the George Washington University Gelman Library. It is a member of the Community of Literary Magazines and Presses and its books are distributed by Small Press Distribution.

wordworksbooks.org

Other Word Works Books

Annik Adey-Babinski, *Okay Cool No Smoking Love Pony*
Karren L. Alenier, *Wandering on the Outside*
Karren L. Alenier, ed., *Whose Woods These Are*
Karren L. Alenier & Miles David Moore, eds.,
      Winners: A Retrospective of the Washington Prize
Christopher Bursk, ed., *Cool Fire*
Willa Carroll, *Nerve Chorus*
Grace Cavalieri, *Creature Comforts*
Abby Chew, *A Bear Approaches from the Sky*
Barbara Goldberg, *Berta Broadfoot and Pepin the Short*
Akua Lezli Hope, *Them Gone*
Frannie Lindsay, *If Mercy*
Elaine Maggarrell, *The Madness of Chefs*
Marilyn McCabe, *Glass Factory*
Kevin McLellan, *Ornitheology*
JoAnne McFarland, *Identifying the Body*
Ann Pelletier, *Letter That Never*
Ayaz Pirani, *Happy You Are Here*
W.T. Pfefferle, *My Coolest Shirt*
Jacklyn Potter, Dwaine Rieves, Gary Stein, eds.,
      Cabin Fever: Poets at Joaquin Miller's Cabin
Robert Sargent, *Aspects of a Southern Story*
      & A Woman from Memphis
Miles Waggener, *Superstition Freeway*
Fritz Ward, *Tsunami Diorama*
Amber West, *Hen & God*
Nancy White, ed., *Word for Word*

Nathalie Anderson, *Stain*
Mel Belin, *Flesh That Was Chrysalis*
Carrie Bennett, *The Land Is a Painted Thing*
Doris Brody, *Judging the Distance*
Sarah Browning, *Whiskey in the Garden of Eden*
Grace Cavalieri, *Pinecrest Rest Haven*
Cheryl Clarke, *By My Precise Haircut*
Christopher Conlon, *Gilbert and Garbo in Love*
       & *Mary Falls: Requiem for Mrs. Surratt*
Donna Denizé, *Broken like Job*
W. Perry Epes, *Nothing Happened*
David Eye, *Seed*
Bernadette Geyer, *The Scabbard of Her Throat*
Barbara G. S. Hagerty, *Twinzilla*
James Hopkins, *Eight Pale Women*
Donald Illich, *Chance Bodies*
Brandon Johnson, *Love's Skin*
Thomas March, *Aftermath*
Marilyn McCabe, *Perpetual Motion*
Judith McCombs, *The Habit of Fire*
James McEwen, *Snake Country*
Miles David Moore, *The Bears of Paris*
       & *Rollercoaster*
Kathi Morrison-Taylor, *By the Nest*
Tera Vale Ragan, *Reading the Ground*
Michael Shaffner, *The Good Opinion of Squirrels*
Maria Terrone, *The Bodies We Were Loaned*
Hilary Tham, *Bad Names for Women*
       & *Counting*
Barbara Ungar, *Charlotte Brontë, You Ruined My Life*
       & *Immortal Medusa*
Jonathan Vaile, *Blue Cowboy*
Rosemary Winslow, *Green Bodies*
Michele Wolf, *Immersion*
Joe Zealberg, *Covalence*

Nathalie F. Anderson, *Following Fred Astaire*, 1998

Michael Atkinson, *One Hundred Children Waiting for a Train*, 2001

Molly Bashaw, *The Whole Field Still Moving Inside It*, 2013

Carrie Bennett, *biography of water*, 2004

Peter Blair, *Last Heat*, 1999

John Bradley, *Love-in-Idleness: The Poetry of Roberto Zingarello*, 1995, 2ND edition 2014

Christopher Bursk, *The Way Water Rubs Stone*, 1988

Richard Carr, *Ace*, 2008

Jamison Crabtree, *Rel[AM]ent*, 2014

Jessica Cuello, *Hunt*, 2016

Barbara Duffey, *Simple Machines*, 2015

B. K. Fischer, *St. Rage's Vault*, 2012

Linda Lee Harper, *Toward Desire*, 1995

Ann Rae Jonas, *A Diamond Is Hard But Not Tough*, 1997

Susan Lewis, *Zoom*, 2017

Frannie Lindsay, *Mayweed*, 2009

Richard Lyons, *Fleur Carnivore*, 2005

Elaine Magarrell, *Blameless Lives*, 1991

Fred Marchant, *Tipping Point*, 1993, 2ND edition 2013

Ron Mohring, *Survivable World*, 2003

Barbara Moore, *Farewell to the Body*, 1990

Brad Richard, *Motion Studies*, 2010

Jay Rogoff, *The Cutoff*, 1994

Prartho Sereno, *Call from Paris*, 2007, 2ND edition 2013

Enid Shomer, *Stalking the Florida Panther*, 1987

John Surowiecki, *The Hat City After Men Stopped Wearing Hats*, 2006

Miles Waggener, *Phoenix Suites*, 2002

Charlotte Warren, *Gandhi's Lap*, 2000

Mike White, *How to Make a Bird with Two Hands*, 2011

Nancy White, *Sun, Moon, Salt*, 1992, 2ND edition 2010

George Young, *Spinoza's Mouse*, 1996

THE TENTH GATE PRIZE

Jennifer Barber, *Works on Paper*, 2015
Lisa Lewis, *Taxonomy of the Missing*, 2017
Roger Sedarat, *Haji As Puppet*, 2016
Lisa Sewell, *Impossible Object*, 2014

INTERNATIONAL EDITIONS

Kajal Ahmad (Alana Marie Levinson-LaBrosse, Mewan Nahro Said Sofi,
    and Darya Abdul-Karim Ali Najin, trans., with Barbara Goldberg),
    Handful of Salt
Keyne Cheshire (trans.), *Murder at Jagged Rock: A Tragedy by Sophocles*
Jeannette L. Clariond (Curtis Bauer, trans.), *Image of Absence*
Jean Cocteau, Mary-Sherman Willis, trans., *Grace Notes*
Yoko Danno & James C. Hopkins, *The Blue Door*
Moshe Dor, Barbara Goldberg, Giora Leshem, eds.,
    The Stones Remember: Native Israeli Poets
Moshe Dor (Barbara Goldberg, trans.), *Scorched by the Sun*
Lee Sang (Myong-Hee Kim, trans.), *Crow's Eye View:*
    The Infamy of Lee Sang, Korean Poet
Vladimir Levchev (Henry Taylor, trans.), *Black Book of*
    the Endangered Species

CPSIA information can be obtained
at www.ICGtesting.com
Printed in the USA
BVHW080816130820
586214BV00002B/167